Field Days

Cover illustration by Hannah Love Shibley.

GRACE PUBLICATIONS
P.O. BOX 18715
BALTIMORE, MD 21206

Printed in Baltimore, Maryland, U.S.A.
Copyright © 2013

Grace Publications is a ministry of
Greater Grace World Outreach, Inc.

ISBN# 1-57907-576-2

TABLE OF CONTENTS

Finland

Sweden

R u s s i a

Germany

Poland

Belarus

Ukraine

Switz.

Hungary

Italy

Romania

Bulgaria

Kazakhstan

Turkey

Azerb.

Uzbekistan

Kyrgyzstan

Turkmenistan

Tajikistan

Greece

PREFACE

This volume represents a collection of stories and messages reported by Pastor Schaller in newsletters he wrote during his days pastoring and traveling the white harvest fields of Eastern Europe, Central Asia and other places. The exchanges cover the period from 1990 to 2003 when Pastor Schaller was overseeing pastor of A Biblia Szol (The Bible Speaks) church in Budapest, Hungary. In Budapest, he co-labored with a very prayerful and very internationally diverse team of dedicated believers who were called to plant churches in places formerly ruled by atheistic communism.

These stories come to you very much as they were written then. They reveal the laughter, the joys, and the tears that come with working the fields of souls. What comes through clearly is a deep, Holy Spirit-inspired dedication to the purpose and plan of God.

A moderate amount of editing has been done for the sake of continuity and confidentiality. We pray that these news reports from Pastor Schaller's "Field Days" will stir your heart to prayer and action in the great call from Jesus Christ to seek and to save those who are lost, here, there, and everywhere.

Pastor Steve Andrulonis

INTRODUCTION

Everybody has a song. Our song is the message of our lives. Jesus Christ made it possible for us to sing a new Song. Psalm 40:2 "He gave us a new song."

The old songs of our old lives have a particular sound. The self-life is stuck in the throat. The minor chord is obvious to those born into major chord living. When we are accompanied by others, the symphony, the chorus of His newness sings loud and clear.

During the years 1972-1975 in Bible school in Maine, we gathered daily and sang our songs. Our Bible-soaked and Spirit-filled pastor invested in us tirelessly and lovingly. We were like a "little flock" that was stirred to believe God with our five loaves and two fish. We prayed and dreamed about going to different parts of the world with the Gospel.

Some of us went to a sparsely populated European country in the north, bordering the U.S.S.R. It wasn't obvious to all of us why we went to Finland, but it was here where our learning was put to the test. Was our song from God or not? Could we live this life of grace and be effective ministers of God's life in a foreign land? The word of grace, the steps of faith, and holding forth the word of Christ personally and practically made a powerful impact.

It was in Finland where our church and Bible School had an effective ministry both in the cities of Finland and in countries behind the Iron Curtain. A lot of ministry happened during those years 1975-1981.

It seemed unlikely at the time that communism would one day crumble. I still remember the day when in Helsinki the "Moscow green train" arrived carrying Leonid Breznev. He came to meet with world leaders and to sign human rights agreements that became known later as the Helsinki Accords.

At the time I was on the streets of Helsinki sharing and evangelizing, oblivious to world affairs. I do remember closed streets and long caravans of black Volgas and the word on the street about the "big guys" in town.

The Russian Bear was strong and continued to loom as a threat to the world politically. Her atheistic ideology was no secret. We were simple common people who cared for the further propagation of the Gospel of Jesus Christ by teaching and making disciples. We were busy in those days both in Finland and across the Baltic Sea in Estonia and in other parts of the U.S.S.R.

During these days, it was supposed that I worked for the CIA by certain elements of Finnish society and reported to be an agent in a Soviet newspaper in Estonia. The affairs, activities and values of our societies are one thing, but the work of God deep in the hearts of people is another. We can say that we live to the beat of Another —we sing a different Song.

It amazes us today—perhaps more than ever —that God did a great work in Finland during these years. Thirty years have passed and more than 80 Finns have been instrumental in church-planting work and ministry in more than 19 countries. We are still singing.

After my family and I left Finland, we pastored briefly in Stockholm before returning to the U.S. to help our home church. In 1989, my wife and I were watching the evening news when we saw and heard that the Hungarians had allowed 30 bus loads of East German tourists to leave the country to Austria—a western country.

This was practically the end of the Iron Curtain.

I knew in my heart that now there was a great opportunity lying before us. There was a door incredibly important now open.

Within weeks a number of us were talking and planning to start a church in Communist Eastern Europe. Pastor Matti Sirvio, a Finnish leader who had already been active in the U.S.S.R. and Eastern Europe, encouraged us to move to Budapest, Hungary, with a team.

He and a team arrived in Budapest in February 1990. My family and I arrived that summer. During the years from 1990 to 2003, I regularly wrote newsletters to a circle of friends, churches and supporters. They contain the elements of our new Song.

We have no message but the person of Christ. There is nothing that ultimately makes sense but He who rose from the dead. All the ways of man are no different from the complete failure of communism.

Today's post-modern ideology will also leave man high and dry. Promises without fulfillment, clouds without rain, trees without fruit, a stranger's voice continues to seduce men everywhere. Those in former Communist countries and today in many Islamic countries are tired of the old song. They have ears to hear who Christ is.

Our prayer is that some people reading this selection of newsletters will be stirred to follow Christ with all their hearts and minds. He is our Song.

I want to thank the people who encouraged me to follow God in this mission work. Particularly, my pastor, Carl H. Stevens Jr., who studied hard and long to give us Bible-saturated and Spirit filled messages. He taught us so much on many levels. I also want to thank my home church and all those who have loved and continue to love the purpose of God as seen in the Great Commission. I also want to thank Pastor Jim Morrison, who first suggested that these newsletters be collected into a book. Pastor Steve Andrulonis picked up the idea and put this together.

Also many thanks to all the servants serving on various fields to make the name of Christ better known.

Pastor Schaller
Baltimore 2007

ENCOUNTERS ON THE STREETS

Fall 1990

On the crowded walking street in Gyor, Hungary, an hour and a half west of Budapest at about 3 p.m. one man said: "The Russians came here and gave us a message and we believed them but it didn't work. Now you Americans are here, should we believe you?"

I answered, "You should believe what I'm saying to you—whether I or a Russian speak it to you—because it is the truth. Communism is a lie and Karl Marx is dead."

I was very bold, simple, and dogmatic. The crowd gathered around us. "Jesus Christ is alive and gives you eternal life. Communism was a message of sociological consequence. This is a message of eternal consequence. Communism was entirely occupied with this life. We are not. We are speaking to you about eternal life."

Another said: "Are you here to save us?" The people were shuffling closer and with craned necks and attentive eyes, they were eager to hear. One man's eyes were very big as he stared, standing quietly at my elbow. People were staring and fascinated. Public speaking on the street with foreigners in post-Communist Europe is a spiritual adventure.

I answered, "No, we cannot save anybody, but God can save you. We are here to sow seed."

The crowd gathers as they hear Americans speaking English and the discussion has a weighty tone.

The crowd is now very interested and there is spirited dialogue in Hungarian with the man who spoke first, comparing us with the Russians.

He answered: *"A Biblia egy tündérmese."*

"This man said the Bible is a fairy tale," I bellowed out to the crowd so all could hear. Ferenc interpreted with a loud voice.

"It has been taught by some that this book is a fairy tale and cannot be trusted. That is entirely not true. I can convince you that the Jewish prophets were inspired by God: 40 men wrote the Bible over 1,600 years—and all of their writings are without contradiction. For example, the prophet Daniel prophesied about the coming Messiah and his death. He predicted the exact date He would die." Then using the sketchboard we taught Daniel's prophecy.

Many people here are fascinated with numbers. In one case a man took out his calculator and computed the 69x7x360 days. He was unhappy complaining that we should use 365 days for a year rather than the Jewish year of 360 days. He was beyond argument, however, but the dialogue touched the "reason of the crowd." This one stayed, with others hurrying along. We then passed around a paper for people to give their addresses so we can send them notifications of our seminars, Bible studies, etc. We collected about 30 names and addresses.

One middle-aged man on the street asked: "What does it mean to have rest?"

Answer: "Our only rest is in God."

"What do you think of spiritists?" another asked, leaning forward with keen interest. We found out that a local newspaper published that a group of Satanists had recently made certain threats.

In the crowd, there was a small number of people

who had received a small amount of false religious teaching. These people usually ask the question: "What is the name of God in the Bible?"

Our answer: "God has many names in the Bible, for example: Adonai (450 times), Zebaoth (230), El (230), Eloah (50), El Shaddai (50), El Yona (32), Elohim (2,570. Yahweh (about 6,000)." I had recently memorized this information so it came in very handy. "And of course in the New Testament: Father, Jesus, Savior, Lord." This answer usually silences them, perhaps instructs them and many prompt stronger reproof from the preacher.

Another interesting and touching encounter was about two weeks later again in Gyor (as we have been going weekly for street work which has now resulted in a Bible study). A sixty-year-old lady with a loud voice and powerful bearing spoke directly to Ferenc.

"When I was sick, I prayed, but God didn't heal me," she repeated with a convicting sense of unbelief.

I said softly, "God loves you," and then, "Please believe me, God really loves you."

And then again, "Please don't be bitter against God or anybody. It does you no good. Believe me, please believe me. Listen really... God has a plan for you, trust Him, He loves you."

She listened and walked away, but several listeners gave us their names and addresses.

Another man, who seemed extremely serious in his thought, came back after listening for a short while about life after death. The question is very commonly asked and interesting to almost everybody. Sometimes we draw a sketch of a dead man and teach on the doctrine of the resurrection including Christ's second coming. Then he asked, "Can somebody who commits suicide go to heaven?"

I looked at him wondering what was on his mind.

"What do you think?" I asked.

"I don't know" he answered.

"Nor do I really know," said I, "but I know that when Christ is living in us by His grace we are fully satisfied with life."

In Budapest, sometimes a certain category of people, usually older unbelievers, parrot their reasons for not really listening. "What do you know, you're so young. We lived through the hard years of communism. You don't know the suffering we went through."

I answered forcefully without a tone of sentimentality, "The Queen of Sheba and Noah and certain Hungarians will rise up in the judgment and testify of how they found God when no one else did—because if you want Him you will find Him. You are without excuse before God."

Another question: "Do miracles take place in your church?"

This question is fun to answer, as it is a good take-off for boasting in the Lord for all His goodness toward us in Christ Jesus over the years—speaking about the history of the church, the suffering church, the millions of believers who know Him and have seen His good hand—and have the high praise of God in their mouths. We also speak a short word on the value of the faith walk as well as being careful to recognize that Calvary and Gethsemane were God's perfect will—not only the resurrection, but also the hours and years without miracles.

Lastly, there is a very precious group, they are the silent listeners with tears in their eyes. The more simply, pure and sincerely you can speak—the better they like it. They can stand and listen for hours. When the Word stops, they leave; but as long as the Bible is taught, they stay. The more Bible, and the more clearly Jesus Christ is pronounced, declared, and made known, the more they like it. They are part of God's chosen for sure. God only knows what races through their minds, having once lacked the Word, and now hear it on the streets. If there is theater, they go away. When speech is trite, or light or stories of a light nature are told—it's not worth their time. But sometimes, when God has the preacher and the Word is flowing, we have seen one or two stand with tears rolling down their cheeks and hands fumbling for a handkerchief. What precious people—only God knows.

A RAINY AFTERNOON IN ESZTERGOM

December 1990

As we sat in the cafeteria-style restaurant, I looked out the large window at the large cathedral built long ago on one of the hills bordering the Danube River. Relaxed and eating lunch with two brothers, my mind drifted in and out about the mini-mission we were on. We were doing something and in Hungary that is inevitable. Wheels haven't stopped turning, nor have they diminished in number. With every new person who gets involved with our church, a new wheel begins to turn; there are new opportunities, more needs to be met, and an increase from God.

As we sat together, my mind savored the view of a huge domed cathedral, the solid rock it was built upon, a small winding shale path zigzagging upward, a small white-washed chapel on an adjacent hill, and a few old cars climbing the road that cuts through the town to the river leading southward to Budapest. Thoughts of villages began to fill in the space down the river between here and Budapest.

It is not difficult to imagine a Hungarian knight in shining armor (about 12th century) perched on a horse traveling through to Slovakia, reinforcing his master's authority wherever he went. I looked down at my greasy kaposzta, thought of my clogged arteries, said grace to myself for the third time and continued to eat with thanksgiving and zeal.

Mushfik, a Budapest Bible Institute student from Baku, Azerbaijan, exchanged a few words with me about the title of the message we were posting in the small city: "How God Turns Beer into Furniture."

"I got the title from a line I read in one of Vance Havner's books," I told him. "Vance Havner was an American preacher." Thinking of how Mushfik's Islamic culture has no bright luminary like Havner, I explained to him a little about American church traditions, preaching and church life. He is growing tremendously in the Lord. I had already preached the message Sunday night in Budapest and liked the title so much that we thought we would make about 50 photocopied posters and post them at bus stops in town.

I looked out the window again and thought of Judit, as I made a giant leap from medieval times to the German occupation fifty years ago. Judit is a forty-seven-year-old Jewish businesswoman who believes in Christ and the Word of God. Her father was apprehended by the Germans and sent to a concentration camp. Miraculously, he escaped, but only for two days. During these two days the man returned home, his wife conceived Judit, he was then recaptured and sent to his death. Some 600,000 other Hungarian Jews died as a result of the German troops and their collaboration with the Hungarian Nazis.

"What have these hills seen?" I thought. Judit has lived her whole life in the shadow of this tragic story. Though she is respectable and has held a responsible position at the National Opera House and has plenty of friends, she still feels that she fears too much. Recently she arranged a meeting in her office with about ten of her colleagues and invited us to speak to them from the Word of God. "We all need to hear and start reading the Bible," she said. "We need God's love, we need courage

17

and care."

Later, she called me and reported that the feedback from her colleagues regarding the study was over-whelmingly positive.

Then I thought of a number of new faces in the church. "Who are these people?" I wondered. What are the stories behind their lives? It is their spiritual hunger, open eyes and the "oil on their faces" that interest me most. We see the evidence of God's work in their hearts, and they are therefore "powerfully disposed" to proclaim the greatness of His salvation to be strong in His grace and not fail or draw back in our call. Look at what He has done!

After a few words, our little group got up from our table and walked outside. It had been raining for about two weeks straight, and the wet, cold air did nothing to brighten the brown, dingy city. But somehow, for me the beauty of Hungary always comes through. The age of the country, its history and size, its talented people, rich culture, its sufferings and oppressions, its geographical location and topography are all so interesting. But many interesting things eventually grow dull and dim.

What is it that keeps everything shining? It's some-thing deep inside the soul. It is these elected ones who have decided to make truth their chief treasure and prize. They make Hungary a trophy of grace, territory to be possessed, celestial soil, a battleground turned sacred. Holiness in the soul makes blessed mud.

We walked to the car, invited a few high school boys to the Sunday afternoon meeting in the local hotel. "How God Turns Beer Into Furniture" will be the topic we told them.

"That's hard," one answered.

"Come and hear," I told him.

He came close to me. "Christ can come into a heart and change a life. Then, the money that once went to the buying of beer is now saved for something more sturdy, something such as furniture." He listened.

We went to the car and jumped in out of the rain as quickly as possible and drove out of town.

Village after village, town after town, city after city, we are planning to evangelize, preach and teach in every possible place by all possible means. Wherever we are welcome, we will try to return. Now we have seven solid fellowships, but of course as always, not enough workers. It is harvest, but not without workers.

Rain was pouring down, *zapor* in Hungarian, a new word for me to learn. We arrived in Budapest for that night of classes. We pulled in front of the large high school where we have our church services and nightly Bible School. "Little steps," I thought as the thought of teaching again that day gripped me. The long view is reached by thousands of little steps. To move step-by-step is all Jesus asks of us. He will do it. He will unfold the long-range goal and purpose. Surely, His testimony is here, in us, and light shines here, and by His grace and our attitude of faith it will never go out...in Hungary nor around the world.

A REDEMPTIVE NEW YEAR

January 1991

My wife, Lisa, and I, in a short discussion before the new year, agreed that we wouldn't look for a "good" new year nor a "happy" new year, but rather a RE-DEMPTIVE NEW YEAR. Men have always lost things (i.e., the Garden of Eden, God, sheep, coins, sons, opportunities, kingdoms, faith, joy—life itself), but God gets them back for us. So surely God will give back to us the things we lose this year.

After we returned from Finland and Sweden—we had unbelievable victories. After our blessed services in Helsinki and Malmo, we returned to Budapest for our third seminar in seven days. When we arrived at home in Budapest, we found out that we had started the new year with Justin's beloved dog lost. What was worse, we had left the dog in the care of one of our "assistant shepherds"—he lost the dog in the village Adyliget, which is spread out widely over the hills of Buda. Added to this was some lost money on the plane. And added to that was the sense or spirit of losing.

We determined, however, to look at the loss in the way we've lived and believed for years: "Lord, we want it all back, everything!" With David as our example (see 1 Samuel 30:6, 19), we believed and started to fight for recovery! After a couple of days, I got all the money back at the airport—Miraculous! And after a few days, the dog ended up at a bus stop sitting under a poster we posted for his recovery. An old couple, without a phone, trekked to a phone booth, made the call—and we got

Bootsie back!

We're still gaining on every count—God is the REDEEMER—whatever we lose. And what about the souls that Jesus sought! They were found.

GOD'S HILL

February 1991

About one week ago, Justin was so thrilled looking out his bedroom window and seeing the street covered with a thick blanket of snow. Our quiet street, which is actually a steep incline of what seems about 35 degrees is perfect for sledding. The hill we live on in Buda is actually named ISTEN HEGY (God's hill). What could be better than living on God's hill (Mt. Zion—note Hebrews 12)! Well, living on God's hill when it's covered with one foot of snow has got to be the best.

Justin (9 years old) said with all seriousness, "They must leave the street like this without plowing it so kids can go sledding." He bolted down the stairs to get dressed, grabbed our landlady's sled, and shot out the door. No plow has been seen on our street, or any other street as far as that goes—and Justin is so happy for the civil authorities in charge, who in their great wisdom and infinite understanding have his interests in mind.

Now our street is a great toboggan sled run. Lisa, passing the living room window through the course of 10 hours yesterday, caught glimpses of Justin's blurred body streaking down God's Hill by himself. He can't stop praising the Hungarians for this great service. It's unbelievable.

Later, at a pizza party with about 50 folks crammed into a tiny apartment, we shared on the subject of "Psychological Security through Spiritual Life and Love." We now see some Hungarians from surrounding areas (up to one hour away) attending services regularly. This is a great blessing, as distance traveled is almost always a good indicator of hunger and, therefore, calling. We're thrilled to see love that moves and travels—we really thank God.

We have seen a few remarkable salvations and deliverances in the past few weeks and a few bodily healings.

Finally, we are learning things about ourselves that we never knew. Two Saturdays ago we were taking a guided tour through one of Budapest's several hundred caves. About thirty of us were in the pack. In the cave we saw various geological formations—and along the way the guide put his flashlight on several bats that were hibernating. We don't know why—there are perhaps many reasons for it—but many of us did feel right at home!

A BOARING STORY

April 1991

A few years, months or weeks from now someone will say, "I am bored."

Somebody standing by might inquire with a wry smile, "Do you mean, you are a 'board' with nails and holes?"

"You've got to be joking," they'll quip, "I mean bored, you know bored." And if I'm standing by I'm sure I'll jump in and say, "Oh that happened to me and a few brothers once when we were driving along a dark country road in Hungary." "What do you mean?" they will counter with stirred interest. Then I will tell this story:

Well, it all started one night after an informal late night fellowship in a country village just twenty minutes outside of Budapest. I believe it was about midnight on a Thursday... or was it a Friday night—oh, I'm not sure... but pay no mind, focusing on details makes everything boring. If I can recall correctly, and I think I do... I've got the watch dial in my mind, it was almost midnight and we were moving right along on a secondary road; riding through the Hungarian countryside. The weather was mild, and springtime was just breaking. Well, you may not believe me but it's true, we passed in the dark shadows a parked car that we later realized had just plowed into a wild boar and two piglets. Well, the piglets would never see the forest again and the huge boar was just a few minutes from kicking its last and serving some higher purpose than just grunting around thrashing through the forest floor, ripping up whatever it can with those interesting tusks.

We pulled the car into position to cast our headlights on its huge woolly body. Some of us were frightened at first. We locked the doors and put our hands over our faces and peered cautiously through our fingers (can't say who...). After a short discussion on the doctrine of fear and automobiles, we boldly stepped out of the car, walked up to it and took turns kicking and poking the beast.

The poor man whom Providence chose to be "His Battle Ax" in ending the life of this boar, walked up to us and started to speak to us in Hungarian (of course, most people in Hungary speak Hungarian). After a few minutes of fuzzy communication, we realized we had an opportunity before our feet. After slight hesitation the three of us turned the prettiest little family station wagon into a temporary wild boar meat transport truck.

We hefted the beast into the rear of the car, and happily returned to the country house we had just left 15 minutes earlier. (We use this house as a men's dorm for five rough and tumble single men.) En route to the house we realized we had a large wild boar in the car. "This is something new for all of us," I said.

We suddenly realized how much fun it was having a boaring time. The three of us dragged the beast thirty yards to the front porch of the house. We stumbled over the carcass in laughter as we dragged it down the muddy pathway. Fresh spring mud, wild boar, and a bunch of Spirit-filled body members in Hungary make for a wild time. We hauled the body to the house and set it on the porch and rang the door bell. From the corner of the house where we were hiding, we studied the faces and action of the men who came to stand before the boar. It was so wonderfully fun watching these men get "boared." Gales of laughter cracked the still midnight air.

There was now quite a bit of circus around this men's dorm. The house is a granite stone house sitting among many others on the side of a mountain overlooking a beautiful valley. Dogs were barking like they always are up and down the valley when they sense midnight activity. Street lights were running the length of the valley for miles. We had no idea who heard us that night as adrenaline was running through our blood in high concentration.

Misha, a Ukrainian brother, was looking at everything quietly with a big smile, perhaps imagining pork steak and chops. Ari offered his plastic raincoat and boots to the butcher. Knives and cords, sticks and imaginative thoughts of where to hang the beast ran through our minds.

I am sure at this point in my story the person claiming to be bored would say, "Sir, I think we have a communication problem. I really don't care to hear more."

To which, I will reply, "I am sorry, but I can only speak of what I've seen, felt, and experienced." With a short bit of enthusiasm and youthful zeal I'll add, "And not only that, but many in the church came that week and ate boar. We had a house packed with people. We all can testify of what it is like to have a boaring time. May I be so bold to say to you, my poor fellow, maybe not all that is right is wright and not all that is boaring is boring."

Chairman of the Boared

THE GREAT TRANSITION

June 1991

The Hungarian Government invited us, and the leaders of about 30 other religious organizations, to the parliament for a get-together meeting. The president of our church, his wife who served as my interpreter, and me, the pastor, found ourselves in one of the most beautiful government buildings I've ever seen. Sitting in a large room with 30-foot-high ceilings and gold paint everywhere made me feel like I could get adjusted to royalty.

One of the Hungarian representatives of the committee stood up and said, "Ten years ago it would have been impossible to meet like this. We could only listen to the words of the priests of the atheists. But now it's possible." We listened to about thirty men introduce themselves to the Committee of Religions and Minorities.

After the short introductions, there was time for comments to be made to the committee. Most of the discussion that followed revolved around the churches getting back those properties that were illegally taken away in 1948 by the Communists. This issue is commonly discussed in the government and an obvious sore point with the people.

I love this country. It once was a huge empire that stretched through central Europe. Providence has reduced its size—but not its soul. I feel that this team, this work, these people who have grown close to our ribs are in the midst of a great work of the Holy Spirit.

God has moved here and is moving. The potential here to help this country in its GREAT TRANSITION to see God establish churches, schools, pastors, missionaries in the ensuing years is incredibly real, extremely important and marvelously precious.

God is with us, best of all, Immanuel! Thank you for your prayers, support, help—we are all on Holy Ground in Christ Jesus. Many of us are broken and awestruck to silence with this oftentimes unbelievable fact that this Holy Ground for us is this extremely effectual work of God in Hungary.

ENCOUNTER WITH A FISH HEAD

April-May 1996 • Tirana, Albania

We stepped into the mosque. The day before, I had heard the "call to prayer" and realized I was really in a Muslim country, or was I? I was in Europe, it did not seem possible that I was in a Muslim country. The mosque sat on the edge of the main square in the small capital of Tirana. The minaret stood up and looked like a concrete missile. An electrical line hung parallel to it with a loud speaker attached. A cassette tape called people to prayer. Men, only men, came in and out of the mosque, took off their shoes and knelt on the oriental rugs. There were no objects of worship in the small domed chapel, only inscription of Arabic on the walls. It felt exotic—maybe Turkish.

It was quiet inside with men quietly coming and going wearing small skullcaps leaving their shoes at the door—reading and/or praying. One was on the side and sat against the wall with one leg under him and the other stretched out straight. Men quietly walked in leaving their shoes at the door and offered up prayer. Albania and Bosnia are the only Muslim countries in Europe.

I enjoy and appreciate any form of godliness. How many people here are searching for God? Like the woman at the well who knew her family tradition, she did not know whom she was worshipping, for Christ said to her, "You worship but know not what" (John 4:22).

I turned and walked out with two brothers.

The white marble helped light up the center of the

city. Spring was still not yet in Europe—we were just four hours by ship directly east from the coast of Italy and one hour flight south of Hungary. It was cold and damp. Downpours for our first two days kept us ducking under awnings, skipping, leaping, circumnavigating puddles and deep potholes.

We slept in a small, unheated, three-bedroom house, the history of which is a memorial to a cruel heartless, Communist dictatorship. Francesko's family lived in this small modest house, in what by European standards was a ghetto area. By Albanian standards, this was a sufficient home. His mother spoke when spoken to, and was eager for communication. We sat every night after we came home from the whole day in the city and ate. An electrical heater heated the living room while the TV fed us news via CNN. Olives, strange smelling cheese, fried fish, bread and more olives were our main food.

We asked Francesko's mother about her personal history. Bit by bit, we understood how difficult life had been in Albania under the most severe form of atheistic Marxism. "My father was a capitalist that came from Italy in 1920. After the war, many Albanian refugees sensed that the Turks could be driven out of Albania so he returned. He was wealthy when he came and within a short time he had thousands of sheep, acres of olive trees and authority over three villages."

During the Nazi occupation and the resistance to it, Hoxha came to power as a Communist. It was in 1944. He was somewhat sensible until 1952 when he became a radical, paranoid, dictatorial Stalinist. He persecuted my family. I am now 50. When I was 12, my brothers, mother and father were taken to a mountain in the south where we were forced to do agricultural work and live in a cave in the mountain. We were refused everything including our rights to make any request for anything. We ate only what the soldiers gave us. We could ask for nothing. The cave had a door built at its mouth. I lived there until I was 20 years old. No education, no rights, and, when my father was partially paralyzed, no medicine, no help." She sobbed. "When my father died, no one was allowed to attend his funeral, only my mother, brothers and myself—no one for he was a capitalist. I worked 27 years and have nothing. I worked twice as hard as anybody I knew."

The next morning we ate fish, bread and olives for breakfast with tea. Cold waters fell from the steel gray sky—cows mooed, roosters crowed, dogs barked in the ghetto for the underprivileged, those relatives of former capitalists, those potential troublemakers, those miserable, poor, powerless, marked ones.

We kissed mother good-bye for the day, walked two steps, opened the metal door and stepped out into the muddy alley that wound its way through the poorest section of Tirana. Ringlets made puddles grow into large pools—periodically a car rolled slowly through followed by horse carts and donkeys.

A crimson rivulet just at my feet caught my eye. I followed it to a hobbled calf nearly decapitated. Oh, I missed the butchering—probably only a few minutes ago. A woman with gold capped teeth flashed a smile and with pride pointed her thumbs at herself, her forearm showing her strength and nodded. I wanted to yell back, my grandfather was in the same profession but we had no time.

I took a few steps, looked back, and the butcher and another woman continued to stare at us—obviously for-

31

eigners, they thought. I played with them by showing mock sympathy for the calf laying lifeless at their feet. Raising my hand to my forehead and looking down and holding a sympathetic pause they caught the jest. I looked up and both women stood staring at me with big smile anticipating more theater. Cross-cultural communication? No problem for those filled with joy.

In the culture house now privatized, the leader refused to receive any payment for using the room for three days. She said: "When we talk about God—we don't talk about money." Four years ago, there were only 1,000 cars and three gas stations and one traffic light in the whole country of Albania. "We need you. Please come here and tell us about your Book."

This morning when I woke up and went outside to use the outside W.C., the scent of firewood woke me to boy-scout days when we slept in the cold and lived in the snow by the open fire for one week. It was cold here last night in Francesko's parents' house. Makeshift mud streets were lined with homemade brick houses, though many are private with electricity. Piles of garbage are here and there in the street, dogs browse through the garbage, as do a small flock of sheep. It has been raining and a cold smoke-screen covers the true wonderful nature of this Mediteranean country.

During the one day we have been here I have not seen anywhere one fat or overweight person. No, wonder, though food is plentiful, the people have lived in hard conditions with tight money, walking a lot and eating healthy meals.

In the process of eating fish at a restaurant, we did an anatomical study of fish heads. I was not eager. Francesko said: "Why don't you eat it?" It was the way he said it—with speed and confidence accented by swift pinch of the lower mandible with his thumb and fore-fingers and popping it in his mouth.

I jumped through that wall of repulsion and disgust for fish heads as if it never existed—Fish heads, OF COURSE! HOW SILLY! Have you ever heard of hamburgers, Kentucky Fried Chicken or tacos?

The lower mandible of the fish broke into tiny bones. I pushed them together with my tongue—and plucked a small pile of slivers out of my mouth looking down at the rest of the head on my plate. I glanced over at Francesko's plate and saw the head was gone when I heard crunching. He nonchalantly plucked something out of his mouth.

With my fork, I extracted one eye—perforated it and out of it popped a very hard, perfectly round white ball. I put it in my mouth and compressed it slowly—it was very firm. I ate the rest of the eye—then started licking and sucking off small parts from the head. Then behind the eye socket I discovered the small brain. I sucked it out—I took off the remainder of the fish skull. I tested its crunch-ability and decided it was not worth it.

My Albanian brother on the other hand ate it—no doubt hard times in Albania taught him much. Actually later I heard that the fish head contains plenty of vitamin B6. Of course, it does!

DREAMS COME TRUE

August 1996

Small Slovakian villages north of the Hungarian border rolled by and the strong trusty Volvo carrying David (Czech), Tamas, Hagi (Hungarian), Amy and I plugged away at its task. Again and again my 1986 Volvo with more that 400,000 kilometers, a vehicle which has seen most of Europe including Cyprus with its previous owner—a missionary living in Hungary—shows no sign of wear. Hallelujah! It is big and strong—loves mission work—it carries us wherever...

"Amy" I said reminiscing, "Eighteen years ago, I was driving south on this road one week after your birth. The day after your birth, I left Finland for Poland, Czechoslovakia and Hungary."

I remember driving in a small caravan of three cars full of Finnish missionaries through the mountains towards Budapest. Through the night, passing slowly through what seemed to me ominous villages, we dreamed.

I prayed one of those prayers you hardly believe, "Lord I would love to come here.... live here.... but how.... it is impossible. This is Communism—real Communism.

"Imagine, Amy, here we are. We live in Budapest and this is ours."

That afternoon our small team stood in the old city of Banska Bystrica—my daughter with me. Possessing the same joy, message and purpose of 18 years ago, we shared the Gospel.

Yes, we dream—and behold reality!

STRANGE AND PLEASANT

August 1997

Here we are at our first Romanian National conference sitting at an old shabby conference building on the slope of a beautiful mountain range in the southern edge of Transylvania. Beautifully sloping mountains, quite high, stand all around us for miles. Large blotches of light and dark greens and steep drop offs plunge down into narrow valleys, rising again to specially signatured peaks. It is beautiful country from mountain top to mountain top as far as you can see.

We trekked up one trail after our afternoon rap to take in the great view and exercise our travel weary and lazy bodies. It was one of the shepherds and hundreds of sheep at the top of roundish and gently sloping mountains that made the view unreal. One flock of sheep here cropping the grass, manicuring the mountain slope and another do their job off in the distance, small white slowly moving dots, dotting the steep slope. Don't they fall? Are they in danger? No, they look as safe, and at peace, and as fitly placed as we could ever imagine—strange and pleasant.

Many things in Romania are strange and pleasant. We, on that mountain top, look east and envision the territory of Moldova and its long and complicated history—torn between Romania and Russia—dull to its constant and laborious poverty, far from vitalization, far from international trade, investment or foreign interest. Dull and apathetic it plods along—"Lord, could you invade these lives with the power and explosion of the

Gospel? Empty the bar rooms, bring fire into the home and hearth bringing singing and vision into the hearts of the young and old."

We look south to Wallenchia, to the plains, the purely Romanian part of Romania. Again, poverty and hardship with barely the infrastructure of a modern nation—a hundred years behind the rest of the western world, with oxen and cart, horse and rider, manually working the field, filthy factories, broken down buildings—houses, roads, water systems all in need of repair everywhere. And the hearts and minds of these people—what is their condition? Surely the Kingdom of God is near the humble broken spirit. Aren't those that are poor in spirit nearest to Christ? Their open hearts are rich soil for words of faith and knowledge of the living Christ who forgives, loves, heals and gives hope.

We look north and west. Mountains roll after mountain until we reach the great Carpathian basin, the Hungarian plains. "Lord, bless our work in Hungary and reach these in Transylvania, Sunday Schools, born-again fathers and mothers, teenagers alert, awake to your grace, your life and purpose. That people would live and walk like Ruth—follow Naomi in a faith vision. When we are persecuted, let us behave and believe like Joseph and Daniel. When we are blind, we will be patient like Paul for three days—when we are under pressure, we will cry to You and you will lead us to a rock higher that ourselves."

The Carpathian mountains make the natural divisions of these parts. Time and the natural phenomena of people, culture forged through all the interplay of migration, opportunities, persecutions, kings, princes, intermarriages between Hungarian-Romanian or Moldovian-Hungarian and seemingly insignificant events like farmer Jancsi losing his cow have made this country a rich mosaic of complicated little histories, and perhaps dangerous hatreds.

Missionaries, like ourselves often know nothing about these things when we enter these territories. We are simply occupied with the fundamental issues of life. Why somebody hates, or is dangerously nationalistic, or narrow minded to the point of never conceiving the principle of faith is not new to us. Naïve to the details, we plunge into the area, with our sketch boards, tracts and rented local meeting halls. We meditate on truths of Christ that have delivered us from the same dangers of life but in another cultural context. Prayer meetings, contagious team fellowship, a relaxed but constant and pleasant sharing of the truths of Christ from Jewish history, the Psalms, prophets, Gospels, Acts, Epistles and the book of Revelation intrigues new and curious people. Truth is the greatest offense to a lie. The way above delivers us from the path of hell below (Proverbs 15:24). Hungry men do not need analysis; they need food.

Though perhaps ignorant, we carry the great message of Christ, the healing of a man, deliverance from sin, birth of true freedom... life. We look down again and see a village. The next day after vibrant, Spirit-filled morning sessions, we ate lunch at small tables of four. The two packed rooms, one of which was used for our meetings, were buzzing with people speaking Romanian, Hungarian and English. The smell of rich cabbage potato soup, sweaty worn clothes, and musty damp carpet lay unnoticeable behind this life-packed room.

People love each other, speak openly, happily, sometimes fervently. One gets up gently carrying a bowl of hot soup, smiling, laughing, all in symphony with scores of other spontaneous simple movements and words of life. Perhaps 120 people are there in total. Most have never been to a conference before. The price for the entire week with food and housing was $40 per person. For some it was a big step to come—but so wonderful, the fellowship of the Finished Work of Christ.

Christ is here in our midst, the seeds planted have grown in the context of details unknown to us—but Christ's life is evident. Shouldn't it be? Life is not polished here. Clothes are worn, hair, teeth, personal hygiene, health care is not what we know in the West. Nutrition, health needs, medicine are definitely lacking. Most people here who have cancer are sent home to die. I was told that half of the people who have an appendectomy here die due to infection and lack of antibiotics.

How many know of personal heartache that could have in another culture been avoided? Is this a time warp or culture warp that we have stepped into? No matter, life is the same, isn't it? Did Christ suggest something different for the 20th century? Or, is His message one way for the Chinese and another for the African? No, unforgiveness and forgiveness, hate and love, unbelief and faith, stubbornness and receiving are not questions of time and culture; they are those elements that either darken or lighten my life and are deeply personal.

After lunch, though it is raining, instead of walking one hour down the mountain to the village, we drive in a few minutes. Some don plastic bags on their heads and walk. One umbrella for a few and others stand in the rain as we plan our village outreach.

We break up in all directions. Small, cute, wooden houses, and cottages line both sides of the narrow muddy street. Warm, friendly people with great curiosity greet us and wonder. Most are Orthodox, but usually answer slowly with a sound of caution. "In the ground" was the answer by two men when asked where will you go when you die. One group, two chaperones and six teenagers, stopped in the rain and listened to me speak to them about Christ. They listened reverently without a word. I continued and felt constrained by the Holy Spirit to pray. Ferenc interpreted—we prayed, they prayed with us without missing a step. There was a wonderful sweetness there in that muddy street in the rain. We bid farewell. Ferenc yelled to them a moment later "Where are you from?" They answered: "On the coast of the Black Sea".

A village in the midst of the mountains—randomly picked out from a mountain top view—we converge on it for a few hours—not knowing the details of their lives, but knowing the power of the Gospel, that Christ is the health of a man's life, the blessing of a family, a village, a nation.

The Balkan region is a land full of such villages—houses and wagons, horses, oxen, sheep, goats, Gypsies, Germans whose families settled in Transylvania in the 14th century, Hungarians, Romanians, small houses made from used stones, bricks and wood; people who love their families, the essence of their survival, their small piece of land, gardens and fences, mostly Orthodox who know much about religion and the cross of 2,000 years ago. These people need the great message of the cross of today, the Christ of this moment who constrains us. Christ came so that God would be with us NOW. Immanuel, God with us. All that God is would be in all that we are—Christ in us... the unspeakable gift.

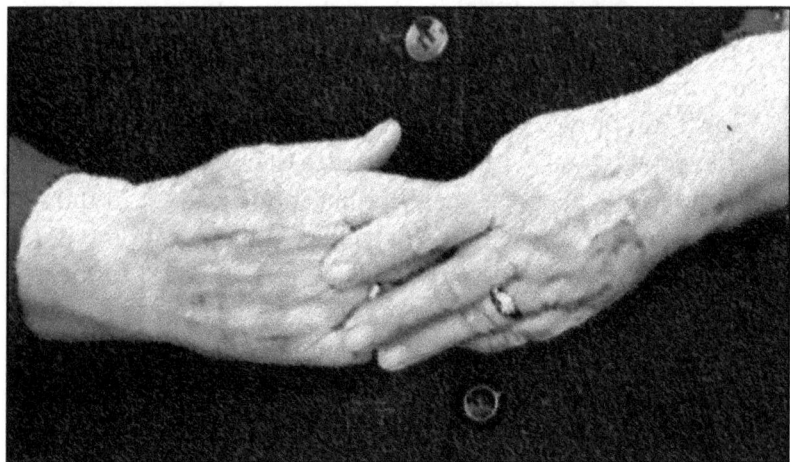

HANDS OF CARE

February-March 1998

Recently in Kiev, Ukraine, when knocking on doors in a typical Soviet-style apartment block house, we met a sixty-year-old woman who came to the door, started to speak to us, and then broke into tears. Oleg and I listened to her story. She spoke with confidence and then brokeness overwhelmed her. "My husband wants me to poison him. I cannot leave him alone. He is partially paralyzed and I must care for him always."

Through the open door behind her, we could hear her husband crying out to her in tearful muffled tones. Then we could hear him shuffling to the door, saying something and then breaking into tears and weeping.

We asked the lady if we could come inside and speak about God to both of them. The apartment was clean with everything neatly in its place. The varnish on the wood parquet floor had worn off years ago. Old electrical appliances with old cords and plugs, like many things in the Ukraine, remind you of those glimpses of life that we got from our parents who lived their childhood in the Depression of the 1930's. Linens, table clothes, tapestries, throw rugs, tables, chairs, lamps were all thread bare, dulled, discolored, worn and old.

They sat on the edge of his bed, as Oleg and I started to explain who we were and what we were doing. We spoke about Christ, God, our loving Father who cares for us. She, sitting next to him, would periodically wipe the tears from his face with her fingers and the palm of her hand. With the big, sweeping, careful and gracious movements of her large, softly padded hands, she cared for her husband.

We ministered to them and with reverential attention, they listened to the Bible. We read it, quoted it and encouraged them.

He spoke, with intermittent breakdowns of tearful emotions, and then immediately came the sweeping hands and hugs of encouragement from his wife. She buried his old head quickly in her shoulder and made tender rebukes. "Stop it," she would say firmly, but with great love and care. Oleg and I sat and listened and watched. We watched every detail. This is life for these two. We were teachers and students simultaneously. We studied and loved these two people facing tough times.

They were both tearful, but those hands of care represented the essence of life. Problems, yes, but life is more than these details. It seemed that behind all of it, there is love. If there is love, there is hope. If God can touch us with His hands, if God cares for us, we can make it... day by day.

Of course, He is enough. We need the simple and real solution for our lives—truth and grace. Perhaps, we will not have this or that—but are not those hands enough for the moment? Aren't God's big sweeping hands enough for us... moment by moment? May God send laborers to the white harvest fields in this world. Let us pray: "Send laborers into the harvest fields with loving hands, big sweeping hands of comfort and love."

DISINTEGRATION OR PERSONAL INTEGRATION

January/February 1999

It is interesting to note there are two distinctively different character sketches in Joseph's biography. They caught my eye the other day while in flight to England from Budapest. The first of these sketches was Reuben. He was the oldest son and therefore the responsible one. He advised his brothers not to kill Joseph. All of Joseph's brothers were jealous of Joseph and conspired against him. Joseph was sold as a slave and brought down to Egypt.

Note one psychological principle at work here in Reuben's life. After their brothers put him in the pit, later Reuben discovers that Joseph is gone.

"And Reuben returned unto the pit; and, behold, Joseph was not in the pit; and he rent his clothes.

"And he returned unto his brethren, and said, The child is not; and I, whither shall I go?" (Genesis 37:29, 30).

Reuben's life was falling apart. "Where shall I go?" was said out of despair, the sense of shame, the desire to run and hide. "If I take the wings of the morning, and dwell in the uttermost parts of the sea" (Psalm 139:9).

These verses refer to man's sense of shame. Shame is from what one psychologist describes as the result of "reality piercing through" my external self to my helpless internal self.

When something happens so that I feel small and ashamed, when I come abruptly face-to-face with the internal self I am hiding, I disintegrate and panic. I feel like Reuben, "Where shall I go?"

Reuben was part of the conspiracy to get rid of Joseph. His small internal self, as seen in the jealousy he had for his brother, was the reason why Joseph was put in the pit. When the plan took on a new twist, that his brother was gone, the reality of what he had done smacked him in the face.

Professor James Gilligan, a criminal psychologist has said, "All acts of violence are motivated by a profound and searing sense of shame. When the distance between my inner self and outer self is great, then there is a stronger sense of shame, personal failure and insecurity. At this point, I disintegrate and feel like hiding or fighting."

Imagine all the violence that occurs in homes and among family members because of shame. The very people we should love the most become victims of our own smallness. When "reality pierces through," when we are guilty and accused by others, when our life disintegrates, we lash out at the ones we love. Often our relatives are present when reality pierces through. They become victims.

**

The other character, who experienced the opposite phenomena, was Joseph.

Joseph had a spiritual life; his walk with God gave him security. Joseph's new inner self (Colossians 3:10) was not far from his outward reality. He was simply one. Joseph was who he was. God was next to him, strengthening him, speaking to him, feeding him. The truth was the key to his life. There was no great distance between who he was outwardly and who he was inwardly. His life flowed with personal integration.

The reality of Joseph's blessing, strength, and harmony with God was seen in the fact that he always sooner or later had keys. All the keys of life are in Christ's hand. He has the keys of grace, the key to every circumstance, the keys to death and hell, and the keys to heaven.

Joseph was a slave, then he was given the keys to Potiphar's house (Genesis 39:3). Then when he went to jail, he was given the key to the jail cells (Genesis 39:21-23). Imagine, a prisoner in charge. Then Joseph was given the position next to the throne of Egypt (Genesis 41:38-40). "Thou shalt be over my house, and according unto thy word shall all my people be ruled," Pharaoh said to Joseph.

Joseph did not sense shame, but honor. Why? Joseph's inner man in every situation was his new self. When "reality pierced through" it found Joseph's trust in God's person. Joseph always reckoned on God's strength, wisdom and grace. This was his identity; it was his life. Consequently, God is the lifter of our head. He feeds the new man, the inner self. God is in us, our hope of glory. Joseph as a slave receives keys.

"There be many that say, Who will shew us any good? LORD, lift thou up the light of thy countenance upon us" (Psalm 4:6).

"I have set before thee an open door, and no man can shut it: for thou hast a little strength, and hast kept my word, and hast not denied my name" (Revelation 3:8).

Paul wrote to the Corinthians that there was a great door open at Ephesus and effectual in 1 Corinthians 16:9. Word of God believers with little strength in themselves have actually great strength in God; a new self, a new inner self. Paul, when he was facing rejection by a segment of the church at Corinth said, "I am who I am by the grace of God." He rejoiced in the law of God after the inner man.

Lastly, the two men Reuben and Joseph can be seen in one New Testament man, Peter.

Peter outwardly confessed his loyalty to Christ. He actually believed he was able, loyal and strong. He even sliced off someone's ear, as a mark of his loyalty and strength. There was, however, a great distance between Peter's outer life and inner self. After he denied Christ three times, "reality pierced through." He went out and wept bitterly, surely thinking to himself, "Who am I? What am I? How greatly disappointed I am with myself."

Christ, however, entered Peter and he walked in his new self. Peter received healing. He was forgiven. He received new counsel, counsel that reinforced who he really was. At the end of his life, he could say with depth and conviction that he really was who he was. He lost his life for Christ's sake on a daily basis by denying himself, and eventually suffered martyrdom. Though he had failed, he received keys. He ministered and doors were open.

We either live in an outer world far from our inner self and periodically sense shame and terrible insecurity, or we receive Christ, walk in Him and receive an open door that no man can shut.

FROM THE SMOKE AND THE RUINS …
LIFE SPRINGS

August 1999

I look out of my fourth-floor office window here in the eighth district of Budapest, and I see an old, large factory complex lying in ruins and decay. Actually a small, low cloud of blue smoke is slowly rising as if there is a little bit of life left in the huge complex.

Dozens of warehouses, thousands of broken windows, rubbish lying on flat roofs hosting weeds and small trees, naked steel girders a mile long, silent space, motionless chimneys, and steel rusted paper-thin covers hundreds of thousands of square meters. The nature of man, of hope and opportunity and the wonder of the free enterprise system that feeds man's natural desire to build, succeed, work and look for opportunity will someday resurrect the destructive forces of an old and inefficient system. The Chinese wholesalers have already started renting a row of warehouses across the street.

We are sitting in a building that was built in 1906 by the owners of that factory. It was a culture house used for baths, haircuts, dentistry, movies, food feasts and the famous steel-men choir—"Aczel Hang korus"—and a score of other purposes. During World War II, it was used as a hospital, and later as a Communist meeting hall. A large bust of Lenin is still in the dark bomb shelter deep in the cellar.

The housing that surrounds the building, 660 apartments, was built for the workers who worked in the steel and machine factory that made parts for the railway. Many apartments are inhabited by the old and the poor, some of whom remember earlier years of busy and bubbling activity in the immediate community called the "kolónia," or colony. All of this died like the factory. This large culture house that seems to be specially designed for our church was sitting empty and useless apart from a few offices and "The Black Hole," a counterculture discoteque in the half basement.

Like the cloud of blue smoke across the street, we are in the building and breathing faith. Workers are putting up walls, renovating and modifying rooms and racing against the clock to get our Hungarian school ready for September. We get our last permit today thanks to a small group of hard working secretaries and planners. Offices and our tape studio are slowly taking shape.

Most of all, our meeting hall is full of life. Empty spaces and high ceilings are filling with the "Immaterial Stuff" that drives out loneliness and fear and unbelief. Love is hope in a horizontal direction. Love is worship in a vertical direction. Love is security in a inward direction. The naked girders across the street, judging from the progress of change in this country will one day be torn down and replaced with something new. Something else is new here now, and we are thrilled.

GENTLE MOVEMENTS IN CENTRAL ASIA

August 1999

My daughter, Amy (18 years old), emptied her bank account and flew to Finland so she could meet me to fly to Uzbekistan. We first flew to Moscow and then to Tashkent to meet the others. Humble, meek people with longing hearts to know Christ met us. The terrain was like Arizona, the system of government and culture was old Soviet. It is always a joy to be moving and living in the consciousness of God's work. Words did flow as if God Himself was speaking gently, patiently and encouragingly to these new believers in Samarkand, an ancient city. Marco Polo, passing through here in the 13th century, reported that one in ten villages was Christian. It is now primarily Islamic-Soviet.

One late night taxi ride across town was memorable. That night we all gathered quietly, under the starlit night, sitting on a large bed like a platform one meter off the ground covered with Asian carpets and pillows, with about 50 chairs around it. In the night like a flow of crystal clear water, we spoke of Christ, heaven, marriage, love and faith. I could not see the faces of the people that night because of the light and its shadows, but I could sense the value of the moment, the authority of Christ in the Spirit, the hunger of these precious people, the presence of God and His angels.

Late at night in a semi-arid land, in a world not clearly known and understood by us, we sit in the midst of newly born sisters and brothers, some of whom we have never known before. In a way that can only be understood by those that know it, we share life, break bread, drink the same Spirit and know Christ in our midst. In the taxi, on the way home we fly. Our speech is like those of the disciples and we dream. We dream about this part of the world, about God's work and His love for these people and this land that stretches further east to China. Yes, Lord, you know all things. We are a small part, but you are with us.

***

Amy and I flew to Baku, Azerbaijan, which is the eastern edge of Europe. I am convinced that a story could be written about our missionaries here and it would be comparable to other heroic missionary stories. It has all the ingredients of faith, patience, sacrifice, courage, love, interesting encounters with government officials and meeting interesting people.

One of these interesting people, Hannele introduced to Amy and me as we traveled to the airport to leave Baku. We met T.T., a 90-year-old woman from one of the most powerful aristocratic families in Baku at the turn of the century. She recounted as if it were yesterday that she and her family were drinking tea in one of their large houses, a house so large it later became a museum. It was April of 1921, at ten o'clock in the morning, when a group of Bolsheviks forced their way into her house. She was three years old at the time. Soldiers with little patience demanded that everyone must leave the house immediately.

She said that her father had his coat on the back of a chair. In those days to go on the street with exposed suspenders was improper like wearing your underwear exposed, but he was forbidden to take anything. The

50

family was then sent to Siberia. They had all of their properties confiscated. Her father was beheaded by the Communists. Her grandfather was responsible for engineering fresh water for the city of Baku. He owned and built half of the city, personally knew the Nobel brothers, had business dealings with the Rockefellers and the Rothchilds and personally paid the Turkish government $9 million in gold to send their army to drive out the attacking Armenians from Azerbaijan, which they did.

This sharp alert and yet blind 90-year-old woman had lived through a unique period of history from the Bolshevik Revolution to the present. She was amazed that at the end of her life, God had brought her back to her beloved Baku. She lived most of her life in Siberia, then in the 1980's, as they saw the changing times, they moved to Ashkabat, Turkemenistan. Then the Azeri government gave her and her two children her grandfather's old summerhouse.

Pray that this lady would have her eyes open to her need for Christ in her life and not believe the lie that God will punish you if you change your religion. Does God enjoy our lives in bondage, darkness, fear and guilt, or did He come so we might be set free?

Christ came with His long arm to reach into our darkness.

INTENSE LIFE

January 2000

Since the New Year, I have been in Rockland, Maine; Budapest, Hungary; Stratford, England; Hilversum, Holland; Bombay, India; and Baltimore, Maryland. To write about these places with the people and sometimes life-transforming occurrences would be awesome. Unfortunately, the pen is not fast and the words get stuck or are never found to aptly communicate what many pastors everywhere are privileged to be part of. The essence of what we see in various parts of the world is that the pastors, their families and church workers are gifted, fervent and true yoke-fellows in this marvelous phenomenon, the ministry of the Gospel. They know, we know, that we are not passive observers, but are actually partaking of life's drama in the unfolding play of life.

Suddenly, in the middle of my part, I am caught off-guard and start weeping having realized I am in the midst of somebody's life. The present moment is a holy moment, a critical moment, and a powerful moment. It is perhaps the most important event in this person's life. The other day, I spoke with a lady here in Hungary who thanked me again for the counseling session we had six years ago when I pleaded with her to leave her extramarital affair. In tears, she told me that her obedience to that word changed her life.

Births, marriages and funerals are part of pastoring people, but there are other realities, such as when someone realizes the importance of Divine truth revealed in the Scriptures by the Holy Spirit. The effect of that reality is powerful and results in a fellowship among believers that transcends to a higher level of understanding. When teenagers know Christ, when young adults decide to concentrate on their studies, attend Bible School and follow Christ, when young couples learn how to live together in the Spirit or elderly people decide to follow Christ in their old age, then there is "Intense Life."

Natural distinctions between classes or ethnic groups are swallowed up in the mystery of the fellowship. Jealousy and envy are replaced with a "fellow-partakers" mentality. We have found a new family, a new direction, and an eternal purpose in God's Son. This is pastoring people on a level that brings great remuneration, one that is spiritual, encouraging, eternally exciting and rewarding.

We dig and search for the history of those servants who found such life in Christ. We find those marvelous stories and devour them. Recently, I read in Oswald Chambers' biography that he left a prestigious university and attended a small Bible School with a handful of students to the chagrin of his family and others that knew him. Yet, the character, the wisdom, the practical counsel and the work that his life added to the church are incomprehensible. Those schools that teach theology and emphasize application are the revolutionary force in any culture. This seems to be the crux of our work around the world: pastors who pastor people; pastors who reinforce the calling in others; schools that educate and emphasize the implementation of the education; people of faith who challenge the intellectual and talented by living in an eternal purpose.

Oh! There is a secret in life and it is Christ.

We are pastors and care for people, but we care for those high and divinely important issues. "Peter, lovest thou me?" Three times, Jesus asked this in John 21. When the disciples could not cast out the demons, He expressed His longing desire—"How long must I be with you?"

"You have omitted the weightiest matters of the law, judgment, mercy and faith" (Matthew 23:23).

Pray for us. Pray for Pastors and Christian workers everywhere that the deep may call to the deep. Pray that the message of teachers and preachers would not stroke the conscience of men, but Christ would purge it. Pray that the truth would not be relativistic to a culture or personal preference, but absolute truth with practical application would be received in the closet and imparted on the rooftop. Pray that the laborer would not tire, but be strong by the Holy Spirit.

"CALL THAT NUMBER"

February 2000

The phone is ringing! The phone is ringing! In the month of February as a result of extensive free advertising throughout Hungary and answers to your prayers, our crisis-counseling ministry has received 2,978 calls in one month! Our computerized data sheet gives the facts:

• We have received calls from virtually every region of the country.

• Actual counselors counsel only three nights a week answering calls four hours each night.

• When counselors are not available, callers have the option to listen to a 1.5-minute Gospel message.

• In the month of February, 2,978 calls were attempted; however because of busy lines, only 1,240 calls were received.

• There were 131 counseling discussions.

The following is a testimony of one caller:

"Once upon a time, there was a couple who really loved each other. They lived happily for 30 years, until one day the husband suddenly died. The wife was left alone with a daughter who was twenty years old at that time. This happened ten years ago.

"Emmi couldn't comprehend it nor believe what had happened. I started to look for God in different churches. For six years I was looking, and I didn't understand why I couldn't find God anywhere. I came out from these places even more sorrowful than before. Then I got so ill that I couldn't even walk.

"Then I stopped looking for God; I became bitter; I lost my hope. One night around Easter time in 1997, I heard a voice saying: "Switch on the TV." I did. And I saw an ad on the screen: 'The Bible Speaks Counseling Hot Line...'

"Someone whispered again: 'Call that number!' I tried for more than an hour until I got through.

"The conversation was a great blessing for me. Now I know that God had a message for me, and He has called me to this church. The very first time when I went to service in the spring of 1997, God touched me and I got saved. I received Jesus as my Savior. It was wonderful. God has held my hands ever since. He leads me, heals me, and edifies me. I'm so happy that I can walk with Jesus. I have received a vision, and I have peace in my heart, though my circumstances have not changed. I'm not alone anymore because the Lord is with me all the time. God is faithful, and He helps in the time of need. I will never forget the number of the Hot Line. Maybe there and then, that call saved my life.

"I am thankful to God for all the trials and all my sicknesses. Because of all my sufferings, I found my God and his Son Jesus Christ. Praise God!"

A WORLD OF CONTRADICTIONS

February 2000 • Bombay, India

The pigs and mud, the green slime on the shallow mud hole, the little piglets and not so small pigs busily rummaging through the garbage on the shoulder of the public street caught my eye and made me stop dead in my tracks.

I stared and found it fascinating. A sow with five, six, seven other pigs were looking rather industrious in an empty lot in some pinpoint of a spot in ever-growing Bombay, India. Sun-dried brown walls, cluttered garbage bags, crushed plastic bottles, and shreds of plastic material that refuses to biodegrade covered the area. People walking with that casual walk with an Asian flow are virtually everywhere. Crammed houses and shanties surrounded the plot of land a quarter the size of a football field. In the middle of the field was a small reddish mud building the size of a large closet with a sign hung on the side of it that read in large, faded letters: "This property owned by ..." The name I do not remember and a telephone number followed.

The large sow was busy in the garbage when we passed the first time and on our return from a bit of child evangelism in the neighboring ghetto, the sow was lying unashamedly and with apparent peace and contentment in the shadow of the small building. I can imagine in the West the owner of such a property would not want to be known for fear of being sued, after all pigs living openly in a residential area are a liability, a health risk.

We do have varying thresholds. Sure, my name can be advertised in a little plot in the middle of a residential area, home to the pigs. "No problem" the Indian world says. The thought that comes to your mind, the westerner, has never entered mine, and vice versa. Though our cultures are different, at the very root of our being is something common to us all. This is one of those very truths that fuel the fire of a missionary theology.

Christ is not ashamed to call us brethren. Third world people would not be ashamed of some of the things we are embarrassed by.

People, people in India, everywhere people, religions and evidences of religions are everywhere. Life and movement, tooting horns, motor scooters, people talking with syllables that nearly get stuck in the belly of their throat and emerge with a pleasant rhythmic cadence that almost makes you want to imitate them. Hustle and bustle, sleeping beggars, tribal people hawking their simple wares, carrying burdens on their heads, making handicrafts as they squat on some busy dusty street for hours. Their workshop is a stone or a brick. Their home is a worn and dirty blanket under a parked vehicle, or a slab of concrete under the stars. This is a land of people, people with spirits and hearts, some in a time warp.

The spark of a fundamentalist religious faction in some small quarter of this vast city could spread to a small neighboring street and result in momentary violence only to retire again to a quiet seething that few know until it erupts again. Like all civilized societies, a thin layer of moral and social life retards our internal restlessness. We do have varying thresholds. In this vast land of 900 million people, there are 20,000 languages,

20,000 various people groups and 300,000 gods. What do people have in common? Reason, sense of humor, shame, fear, guilt, a need for security and significance.

Christ's humility and obedience are the keys that unlock a world that had been closed to us. His obedience, by the Holy Spirit in thought, word and action, resulted in an open heaven and closed hell for the believer. When Christ was on earth, He did not venture into the Holy of Holiest in the Jewish Temple in Jerusalem. He only stepped into the temple court.

What humility, being of the tribe of Judah he was not allowed into the holiest places. He did not enter a material building on earth to prove Himself. Because He entered into heaven, He could now enter into an Indian heart anywhere on the earth, at any time.

How different is Jesus from the Antichrist who reigns in the great world tribulation, makes his way in to the Jewish temple in Jerusalem and sits defiantly on the Mercy Seat. "Who opposes and exalts himself so proudly and insolently against and over all that is called God or that is worshiped, [even to his actually] taking his seat in the temple of God, proclaiming that he himself is God" (2 Thessalonians 2:4, Amplified).

Christ delivers the "Big Package" for all men everywhere. That is why we can go anywhere. Our missionary theology is awesome. We have it all! Religion and cultural relativities are not why Christ came. Nor can they hinder Him in His great work. He came to do the "Big Thing"...to bring God to us and us to God.

WHAT IS MUD MONTH?

April 2000

It is the month of April in Hungary. It is the month when we step into villages within two hours of Budapest with the purpose to evangelize. It is the month of deliberate and calculated sacrifice to work for Jesus Christ.

It is the month when we liken our evangelistic effort in villages "where no white man has ever been" as throwing mud hard at a wall. Some of the mud sticks but much falls to the ground leaving mud stains. Some of our evangelistic efforts will stick. Our going enthusiastically, boldly, and prayerfully together by van or other means of transport to a village is an exercise of faith.

We are cutting down trees to expand our inheritance, Joshua 17. We are deliberately working in order to bring a cripple through a ripped up roof so Jesus can see him and perhaps speak to him.

Practically, what does it mean: Team members will make a commitment through the month of April to leave directly after school to seek the lost in nearby villages. Without changing clothes, showering, shopping, or deliberating on questions of reason or pontificating on the use of steroids in beef cattle... we are going to SHARE OUR FAITH IN JESUS CHRIST IN VILLAGES.

Our spirit is we have prayed and we are going. If the van breaks down, we're walking. If there are no interpreters, I will use my dictionary. If I am exhausted, Jesus Christ will quicken me (Romans 8:11). If my feet hurt, I will crawl. If no one listens to me, I will keep going. Zacheus is in a tree somewhere. If I am bit by a dog, I'll bite him back. If my leader is confused, I will go with him, with Him each step of the way. If my first time doing this was a disaster, I will do it every day afterwards until the devil is ashamed he even tapped on my shoulder. I am an overseeing missionary. I eat giants for breakfast. I long for mud on my shoes, souls in heaven, teenagers found by us. They find us and years from now, they will be treading the hills of Kazakhstan or Africa because you went. MUD MONTH—THE BEST MONTH OF THE YEAR.

Various strategies: Each team can discuss strategies and small groups of two or three cars can decide what they want to accomplish.

Blitz strategy: moving fast through the village with the purpose of distributing a lot of literature and making note of the hottest contacts. Going door to door with a goal of "moving right along," leaving a tract at a door where there is no answer and speaking directly, kindly, patiently to whoever is interested.

Investment strategy: spending time with people at a local büfé or kocsma (small dark smoky bar rooms inhabited by people with pickled brains—administer "shock therapy" by preaching to them that they should follow Christ and you right out of that place and go to church that night) is useful and thoroughly enjoyable if they will listen. It may be that they have rarely met a foreigner who would talk to them. Teenagers are great targets.

If you get inspired, offer to return and teach "One Hour of English from the Bible" in the very place you met them. Or invite them to church service in Budapest to meet your friends. "My church is awesome, you must see it at least once in your lifetime. It is at Gutenberg Épület...."

Street ministry strategy: guitars, singing, sketch-board, theater, mime, etc., may be used as God leads. Small theatrical tricks may be used to draw attention to yourselves so that we may draw their attention to

1. Our church
2. Our services—crisis counseling
3. Our faith in Christ
4. Our desire for them to believe—to come along.

Village life may be quiet and people reserved; it may be best and most effective to go through the village door to door rapidly taking note of interested people. Go back next week and invest.

Village size: Some villages are small with 300 houses; others have 7,000 people or more. The driver of the van can give you a general picture of the village and discuss what the intended goal can be for the afternoon outreach.

Enjoy yourself: Spiritual life and fellowship is at the heart of what we are doing. Spiritual life is contagious; enthusiastic faith and love for people is refreshing. May God bless our labors—the fruit of our hands.

THE CLOSET, THE TABLE, THE TOWEL

September 2000

The closet, the table, and the towel represent three different personal disciplines in the believer's life. Like three legs on a stool, they are all needed. One is used to help the other. They all function together for a higher purpose.

First, the closet is mentioned in Matthew 6:6: "But thou when thou prayest, enter into thy closet, and when thou hast shut thy door pray to thy father which is in secret and thy father which seeth in secret shall reward thee openly." The closet is where the believer learns the inner disciplines of the Christian life; prayer, worship, meditation and solitude.

Secondly, the table is mentioned in John 12:2-3: "There they made him a supper and Martha served; but Lazarus was one of them that sat at the table with him. Then took Mary a pound of ointment...." If we have been in the closet, then we also should sit at the table with valuable speech. At the table we speak, listen, comfort, and encourage using our "outer disciplines of speech and personal ministry." Learn the invaluable art of spiritual fellowship. Rap sessions after church services are a great opportunity to fellowship at the table.

Thirdly, the towel is the outer ministry of doing. "Jesus knowing that the Father had given all things into his hands, and that he was come from God, and went to God; He riseth from supper, and laid aside his garments; and took a towel, and girded himself. After that he poureth water into a bason, and began to wash the disciples' feet, and to wipe them with the towel wherewith he was girded" (John 13:3-5). Though Jesus Christ had a ministry of prayer in the closet and a ministry of fellowship sitting at the table, He also had a ministry of service by washing the feet of the disciples, Judas Iscariot included. The outer disciplines of serving people may include feeding the poor, teaching children, helping the unfortunate, swinging a hammer, visiting the sick. Jesus took a towel and knelt down and washed feet. He was not talking and He was not praying, per se, but He was serving. We rise up from the table and go. We serve others in humility.

All three aspects characterize the life of a believer/ follower and one part fits with the others and all are important. If I serve but do not have a closet, I burn out. If I sit at the table but do not pour out, I will lose the joy and refreshment that comes from obedience. If I talk at the table, but do not have a prayer life, my words will lack divine content. If I have the closet, but not the table, nor the towel, then I turn morbidly inward and become conscious of my own spirituality, rather than living with a purpose for others. The purpose of the stool is that we would have a balanced life that is glorifying God and touching others through our healthy self.

Consider this poem:

Others

Lord, help me live from day to day
In such a self-forgetful way
That even when I kneel to pray
My prayers shall be for others.

Help me in all the work I do
To ever be sincere and true
And know that all I'd do for you
Must needs be done for others

Let "self" be crucified and slain
And buried deep and all in vain
May efforts be to rise again
Unless to live for others.

And when my work on earth is done
And my new work in heaven's begun
May I forget the crown I've won
While still thinking of others.

Others, Lord, yes, others.
Let this my motto be
Help me to live for others
That I may live like thee.

C.D. Meigs

Jesus Christ in His life had all three—the closet, the table, and the towel—operating in dynamic relationship. He was with the multitudes, but also separated Himself to prayer and privacy. He often spoke and taught His disciples (at the table figuratively) and traveled constantly to seek the lost (the ministry of doing).

In Budapest we are thinking and moving in this dynamic balance. What a joy!

THE GREAT WORKS OF THE LORD
April 2001

In India after the brutal death of an Australian missionary and his two young sons, the wife and mother forgave the guilty people responsible—now in India the idea of absolute, unconditional forgiveness is connoted by her last name: Staines; i.e. "You are doing a 'Staines.'"

One man in Morocco, after receiving Christ, laid in his bed one night filled with joy and wrote to Pastor Scibelli thanking him, explaining, "Jesus Christ is so real."

A young Bible School student in Romania sensed a strong urge to immediately go visit an elderly lady she had met weeks earlier. The student who was going about her normal routine dropped what she was doing and literally ran through the city and entering the apartment found the lady hanging from the end of a rope in an attempted suicide. She took her down saving her life, and brought her to church where she has found Christ.

Years ago in Helsinki, Finland, a small team of Noah's Ark Bible Club workers turned the corner of a building entering the courtyard to see a lady hanging upside down by her leg from the fourth-floor balcony. She had leaped from the fifth floor only to be caught by the next floor's balcony railing. They contacted the police and prayed for the lady. There are many stories of God's good work.

In Budapest, one of our people was diagnosed with a large tumor that required surgery. After prayer and before surgery, the doctors examined the patient and could not find the tumor.

We had our European Conference in Finland in the beginning of March. Russian, Azeri, Uzbek and Kyrgyz pastors and servants came and could bear witness to scores of similar works of God. All of us have a sense of God's abounding goodness toward us. "The works of the Lord are great, sought out by all those that have pleasure therein" (Psalm111:2).

If the Gospel is the power of God unto salvation and if Jesus Christ gave His believers the great commission, then consider the following. Recently, in the news we've read about a severe drought in Afghanistan that has caught some people off guard. Some village people are stranded in new deserts, refusing to leave their homes. About 700,000 new refugees are migrating to Pakistan with hopes of finding food. Ten years ago, a Russian military helicopter crashed in a lake, 130 feet deep. Now you can see the helicopter and skeletons of the crew in the dry lakebed. Poor, starving people are making the cold trek over mountains, some freezing, particularly children in the back of packed transports.

Afghanistan is a closed, intolerant country to the Gospel.

Is the Lord moving people out so they may hear the Gospel of love and grace in neighboring Pakistan? One of the main elements in our work is from Paul's statement: "I do all things for the elect's sake." Isn't it sure that some of these people are God's elect and it is our place to pray, plan and go to reach them with an act of kindness, with care, love and, if the door is open, a unique and powerful message that has affected others around the world?

In 1979, we went to Communist China. We started

a correspondence Bible School in Moscow in the early '80's. We moved to Budapest within months of dissolution of the Iron Curtain. By God's grace, His people have ventured to nearly every country in the world with the message of God's love, Christ's resurrection, ascension and personal gift to whoever believes.

Let us pray now for Afghans, a people group that has been at war for more than 30 years, oppressed by severe fundamental Islam, where women cannot have a normal education, nor work and men must live by the letter of Islamic law. Isn't it possible that there are Corneliuses praying to know God—and yet have not heard of His grace, and truth? (See Acts 10.)

Surely, Lord, send.

Send, and with wisdom make the way for these dear, needy people to know Jesus Christ. Amen.

BROKEN TO SHIVERS

August 2001

I am ever thankful that God has allowed us to continue up to the present with some rather profound and touching thoughts. I just returned from Europe after visiting and ministering in six countries, four of which were seminar conferences. In the midst of these conferences, God touched us and moved us to address underlying issues of importance, unresolved tensions and lead us in clear thinking—even more, not only good, solid thinking, but glorious thinking that through the Holy Spirit magnifies Jesus Christ. Glorious thinking illuminates the mind, heals the emotions and restores hope. It is inevitable that in the process of meeting hundreds of people, we will meet those shattered and ripped apart.

The Greek word in Luke 4:18 for "brokenhearted" has been explained to me as meaning "broken to shivers." Christ states in that verse, "The Spirit of the Lord is upon me, because he hath anointed me to preach the Gospel to the poor (powerless to accomplish an end), he hath sent me to heal the brokenhearted (broken to shivers), to preach deliverance to the captives and recovering of sight to the blind (blind, mentally blind), to set at liberty them that are bruised (break in pieces, shatter)."

We realize that Christ's ministry on earth as seen in the Gospels is full of this deliverance for the delivered prostitutes, the healed bodies of the leper, paralytic, and bleeding, the delivered demoniacs who were bent on self-destruction, and the humbled proud, all of whom were acted upon by Christ through the Holy Spirit anointing.

The fresh sense of Christ today here, never changing, but caring for these people and on the move in our midst, no, even in our bodies, our hands and eyes, our mouths makes Paul's words light up; "Who also hath made us able ministers of the New Testament, not of the letter, but of the Spirit, for the letter killeth, but the Spirit giveth life." And "Let a man so account of us as of the ministers of Christ and stewards of the mysteries of God" (1 Corinthians 4:1). And Jeremiah prophesied: "And I will set up shepherds over them which shall feed them: and they shall fear no more, nor be dismayed, neither shall they be lacking, saith the Lord" (Jeremiah 23:4).

We could visit a tribe in India, like the Korku people, poor and of very low caste. A Finnish missionary asked one man from this tribe in his native language, "Are you of this tribe?" The man looked down at his feet and confessed with low self-esteem, "Yes, I am of this tribe." Could such a man be restored to the high status of God's son? Could such a man be enlightened? What do the Scriptures say?

On two occasions during this summer, once at our conference in Hungary and once at our conference in Finland, we had missions marches. These marches touched me—the quiet but sure footsteps, the sense of joy that this is a worthy cause, the beholding of the faces of scores of people (but wanting to look slow and long at one face at a time); the thought that some of these are treading on new territory by precious faith in God, and some have labored in great straits for years. Then, the knowledge that some have found an incredible secret about life—and they have a great calling; and then the thought that perhaps we have just started. One life may represent the sweet release of 1,000 people, and all of it was incarnated before us. Are there yet thousands more, and each life of inestimable value? Are these souls in heaven; is this labor in vain; are these thoughts in the Scriptures merely platitudes, bits of worldly wisdom, good stuff for poetry, or songwriting? No! We are leaning with all our weight on them! Like a man in a harness attached to a cable hanging from a rescue helicopter, we are literally throwing all our lives on the words and thoughts of Jesus Christ.

Our religion is not an abstract reconstruction of events 2000 years ago, but the very reality of God in the present because of His Son's life and ultimate and consummate victory over ourselves and all that the old creation is. The words of Jesus Christ now take on real life dimensions. They are conceived in our hearts and minds and ultimately manifested in the dimensions of "lives changed."

THE DIVINE MOSAIC
March — June 2003

I am convinced that there could not be a greater sense of being than to be a channel of thought, feeling and will in the communication of God's word. There is a special quality of thought that comes from the prayerful and anointed presence of the Gospel that exalts Christ's person, work and purpose. Continually through this spring, I stood and marveled at the awesomeness of the message, the profundity of its consequences and the reality of its Person. Wow!

In a kaleidoscopic mosaic of cultures and world views in the West, Eastern Europe and Central Asia, I cannot help but see this again and again. Here is list of my travels in order since March: Budapest, Hungary; Istanbul, Turkey; Baku, Azerbaijan; Almaty, Kazahkstan; USA (Baltimore, Rockland, S. Portland, Dover Plains, Rome, Tacoma); Budapest; Tirana, Albania; Budapest; Sophia, Bulgaria; USA (Westfield); Budapest; Warsaw, Poland; Vilnius and Klaipeda, Lithuania; Kaliningrad, Russia; Cracow, Poland; Budapest; Baku, Azerbaijan; Budapest; and USA (Baltimore, Rome).

Interesting encounters abounded. On the street in Sophia, I met an Afghan who was drawn by the words and life of our 40-person team. "I was nine years old when the Mujahedin murdered my mother and father. My brother and I went to Pakistan, then Iran, now I am here."

"When did you accept Christ?" I asked recognizing he was a believer.

"Eight months ago," he answered. "I want to learn the Bible."

On the streets in Albania, we did sketch board with a mosque in the background. Arguments break out and excited words race through the group. We felt the tension, only to be subdued by a soft answer and God's wisdom that makes people think.

In light of the reality of Christ in ministering, I sometimes step back and remember life without this foundation. There is value in running this race with God. University students who ask questions but rarely hear the Gospel are of great interest to me. Some of them have open minds. Chesterton said that an open mind like an open mouth does have a purpose and that is to close upon something solid.

When we speak with solid thought about life the value of man, the reality of God, the need for forgiveness, the equipping of the believers, the existence of evil, the inevitability of judgment, and the redemptive work of Christ and the assurance of Christ's resurrection historically and as predicted by the prophets, then those minds become salt for Europe and Central Asia and for the world.

A mosaic of people, cultures, personalities and changing national and personal histories becomes the fertile ground for the incredible reality of Christ in the NOW.

To witness this is such a privilege.

POSTSCRIPT

Whenever I left the USA and traveled to Hungary, I had an ache in my heart.

I compared it to doing what was unnatural, as with the milk kine in 1 Samuel 6:7-12 who left their young and brought the Ark back to Israel. The cows were "lowing" as they went. They wanted to return to their young, but the Holy Spirit would not allow them. Two natures were at work—one inclined to care for the young, the other on a mission to do God's will.

I boarded the plane with fresh thought regarding my wife's sacrificial life, love for God, for me, for our mission, and love for our children. I wanted to go home and be with them, but I was on a mission. People leave home for oil, or money, or for war. We do this for the Gospel.

I thought about my family. On the plane, I was lowing. I hope no one heard me. On the other hand, I could care less, I was hurting.

I would have a picture in my mind of the face of my little son Kyle. I longed for the joy of interacting with Bethany and Amy, my daughters, and missed dealing with their lives and enjoying their growth. Of course, I missed the unparalleled comradeship of my teenage son, Justin, who enjoys all those things I enjoy. He is a source of unending joy and pleasure for my life. I have serious anticipation of his future as he grows up to be a young man and, hopefully, lives this life we are now living.

With all of these thoughts, however, there was coupled a fervent prayer in the fiber of my soul. I deeply considered the upcoming weeks and wondered how I would make it. But it was not long before the flow of the church activities and the deeply satisfying relationships with the Hungarians and the team members so stirred me that my heart was mollified by the vision, the excitement, the growth, and the maturity of the congregation. I remember coming home from my Bible College class, which was always very richly edifying. I felt its comfort.

I realize afresh right now that the human heart is capable of both pain and healing, of aching and comfort, and that the human heart is also deceitful and desperately wicked. I therefore know that the ache in my heart cannot lead me. I therefore always have committed my family into the hands of God again and again. He has led me in the judgment that this life that I am living is being lived according to His will, and He is able to both satisfy us at this moment in time and then reward us and deal with us according to His great graciousness regarding the future.

The following could be called our family mission statement, which I wrote once after arriving in Hungary following a sad flight across the Atlantic, I believe, in 1994.

> *Like everyone living life in all circumstances, we all wonder what tomorrow will bring. I have decided to put on paper clearly our family mission statement. What is the purpose of our family?*
>
> *Whatever the future will bring, I have determined to believe that my wife and I have made the right decisions in our calls before God. We are being greatly comforted and encouraged and that in checking our hearts and our motives, we are fully persuaded that*

what we have done has been done because of one reason—and that is because we believe Jesus Christ is the Savior of the world and there is nothing more important than His person and the Gospel.

We believe Christ and His Word. He said, "Verily I say unto you, There is no man that hath left house, or brethren, or sisters, or father, or mother, or wife, or children, or lands, for my sake, and the gospel's, but he shall receive an hundredfold now in this time, houses, and brethren, and sisters, and mothers, and children, and lands, with persecutions; and in the world to come eternal life" (Mark 10:29-30).

More than the consequences that can be measured, we are called to know the Person which cannot be measured.

For thirteen years my family and I have seen God go beyond our expectations in regards to showing us the faithfulness of His character. He has promised and He will do it. All glory to God!

www.ingramcontent.com/pod-product-compliance
Lightning Source LLC
Chambersburg PA
CBHW071341290326
41933CB00040B/1956